The Saint of the Impossible

Everything You Wanted
to Know about Saint Jude

BRIAN MORGAN

A Story That's Never Been Told

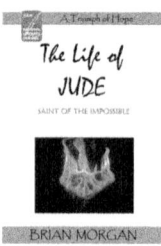

THIS IS A companion book to the author's major work, *The Life of Jude: Saint of the Impossible*. Jude was a cousin of Jesus Christ and the most obscure of the twelve apostles. He is known around the world as the Patron of Desperate Cases, the Hope of the Helpless, the Saint of Last Resort, the Help of the Hopeless – and more.

Brian Morgan spent 50 years researching and writing *The Life of Jude*, a critically acclaimed biographical novel, but there was much information that was not appropriate for that book. This book solves that problem and presents answers to the questions believers have asked about Saint Jude for a long, long time.

Information about all of Brian's book are detailed on his website at www.brianmorganbooks.com. And readers are very welcome to contact him personally by email at:

brianmorganbooks@gmail.com.

The Saint of the Impossible

Everything You Wanted
to Know About Saint Jude

BRIAN MORGAN

THE WRITERS TRUST

Dedication

This book is dedicated to the millions of people around the world, who, in times of desperation and despair, have turned their prayers heavenward in the hope of finding Jude. May you find him in the pages of this book and may your prayers be answered.

Award Winner

The Life of Jude: Saint of the Impossible has won the prestigious Fellowship of Australian Writers' National Literary Award, the Jim Hamilton Award. This award was open to all books in any genre, including books of poetry, whether published or unpublished.

"The oppressed look to him and are glad; they will never be disappointed. The helpless call to him, and he answers; he saves them from all their troubles. The Lord is near to those who are discouraged; he saves those who have lost all hope."
Psalms.

"It is St Jude's special mission to help you when you despair. He helps you see the light that shines on in the darkness - always - and which the darkness can never overcome."
From the Franciscan Shrine to St Jude, Mt Vernon, New York.

Table of Contents

Author's Note

EVER HAD the feeling someone was leaning over your shoulder, watching everything you did? That's what it's been like while I spent 50 (yes, fifty) years searching for the elusive Jude. I had the feeling he was right there all the time, watching.

A bit daunting, really, but, clue by clue, I assembled the dossier that answers questions believers have asked for two millennia.

Putting the book together has involved intensive detective work, many blind alleys, and all the triumphs and frustrations to be expected when delving into such an obscure life, lived so long ago.

It didn't help when I lost all my notes in a house move after 30 years and had to start again.

It seems everyone has heard *of* Jude, but few have heard anything *about* him. He has been a real mystery, an enigma. One nun I spoke to actually believed he was a woman.

"Oh, I love Saint Jude," she said. "I think she's wonderful."

Research has been difficult. No two historians or theologians seem able to agree on many aspects of the birth of Christianity. Information has been hard to trace and very often contradictory. Both the history of the times and the legend of the saint have been hard to pin down.

I was often told the story of Jude's life would always remain unfathomable and should not be written anyway.

The Most Valid Path

While history and tradition vary with Jude, as with most saints, I have stuck to what I consider to be the most valid path of his life, as detailed in my major work, *The Life of Jude: Saint of the Impossible*, which is available online in paperback and eBook formats. It's a biographical novel based on Jude's extraordinary life.

The story of Jude's missionary journeys in this book is taken from that source, although it was gathered from hundreds of prior sources.

For the sake of simplicity, I write as if Jude's mission was one long journey, whereas, in fact, he crossed his own paths many times.

On foot, or by donkey and occasionally by camel, this man of God spread the seeds of the Christian faith through what is now Jordan, Israel, Lebanon, Syria, Turkey, Armenia, Georgia, Southern Russia, Azerbaijan, Iraq, Iran, Afghanistan, Pakistan, India, Saudi Arabia, Yemen, Oman, Egypt and Libya.

Fine details of this book may be disputed - most things are debatable and debated about the origins of Christianity - but I believe this to be as true a story as fragmentary history and legend will allow. Christians will understand if I say that I will have no problem looking Jude in the eye when we finally meet one fine day.

During my years as a newspaper and magazine editor, I was often asked for information about Saint Jude. People particularly wanted to know how to compose words of petition or thanks for the Public Notices section of the newspapers.

This book is a more complete answer than I was able to give at the time.

Brian Morgan

Introduction

WE LIVE in desperate times, when tragedy lurks in the shadows and hope is often an elusive will-o'-the-wisp.

Around the world, millions, literally millions of people pin their desperate trust in Jude when anguish strikes and all else fails.

People might be deep in the mire of despair... they might even have lost faith in God. Then someone might whisper: "Have you heard of Jude?"... And touch a spark to lost hope.

Hope, they say, is the only thing that stops a heart from breaking - and, for many Christians everywhere, the final custodian of hope is Jude.

Why is this so? Why did Jude - a cousin of Jesus Christ and the most obscure of the Twelve Apostles - become known as the Saint of the Impossible, Help of the Hopeless, Hope of the Helpless, Patron of Desperate Cases? Why is he known as the Patron Saint of the Outcast, the Saint of Last Resort, the saint of the homeless, the hapless, the hopeless?

Pick up any newspaper and chances are there will be prayers of petition or thanks to Jude. Check the Internet and discover the extent of devotion to him. Visit a Jude shrine and sit and watch... you will see a procession of the broken-hearted reaching out in desperation.

Some condemn the idea of seeking God's help through an intermediary. But they have little understanding of the timid, the exhausted, the frightened, the sick, the embarrassed, the lowly, the humble.

To those who feel a long way from God, an intermediary such as Jude - especially Jude - is the only way to approach the Almighty.

This little book is a pilgrimage to discover Jude, the Saint of Lost Hope, the man who fanned the flame of hope two thousand years ago and who fans it still.

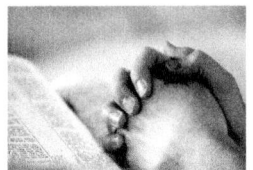

Who was Jude?

JUDE WAS BORN in the year BC8 at Panias, which was called Caesarea Philipi by the Romans, and is now called Baniyas, in Israel. He died a martyr at the age of eighty in AD72 at Susia, in Persia (now Iran).

As can be seen from the family chart (next page), he was a cousin of Jesus Christ and a brother to two other apostles, James the Less or James the Righteous and Simon. He was also related to two other apostles, James and John, the sons of Zebedee.

They were all Jews who had a wide knowledge of the Bible and of Jewish Law. They were devout men. They followed their Master, Jesus, for three years of preaching and healing and miracles in Judea and Galilee.

That story is told in the New Testament.

Jude's family owned olive groves and supplied

Family Chart

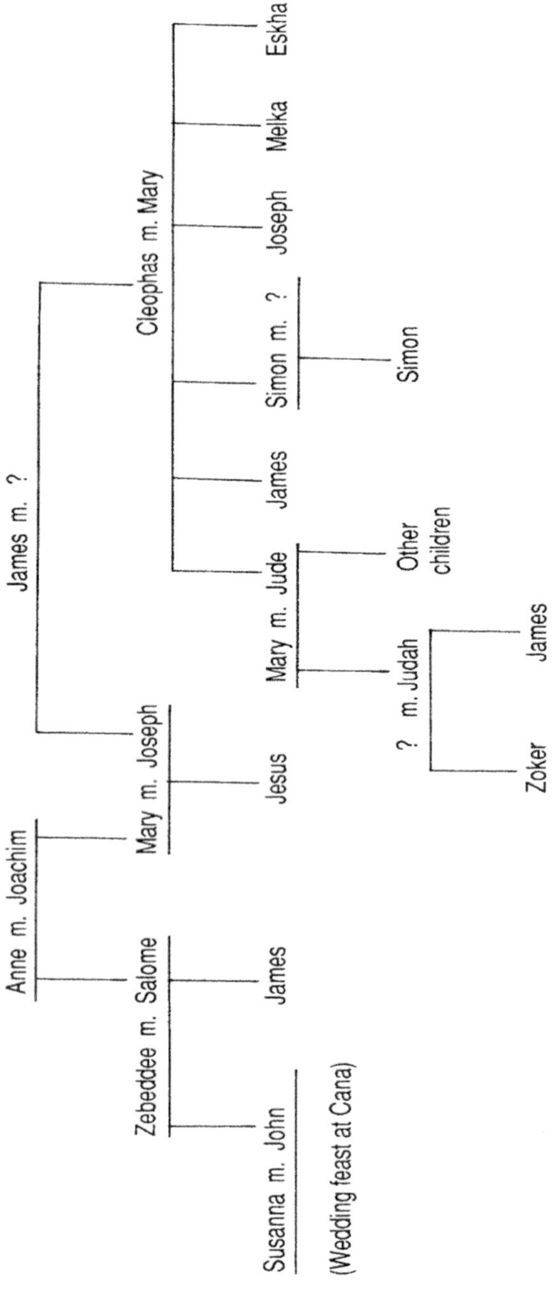

```
Anne m. Joachim
        |
   -----------
   |         |
Zebeddee m. Salome    Mary m. Joseph ----- James m. ?
   |                      |                 |
  James                  Jesus     -----------------------------------------------
                                   |        |       |        |            Cleophas m. Mary
Susanna m. John              Mary m. Jude  James  Simon m. ?  Joseph   Melka   Eskha
(Wedding feast at Cana)           |                  |
                          ? m. Judah  Other        Simon
                            |        children
                       ----------
                       |        |
                     Zoker    James
```

olives and olive oil to many parts of the Mediterranean world, then part of the Roman Empire. The oil was used for lighting and cooking, in perfumes and medicines, and to anoint Kings and priests.

Jude is believed to have worked also, at times, with his cousin, Jesus, in Joseph's carpentry trade at Nazareth and also with the fishermen on the Sea of Galilee.

Cleophas, Jude's father, had lodgings in Egypt to carry on his oil business and legend says it was to these lodgings that Joseph and Mary took the infant Jesus when the baby's life was threatened by Herod.

Jude spoke Aramaic and Hebrew and also Koine, the Greek language used particularly for commerce throughout much of the world at that time.

An Extraordinary Life

His extraordinary life as one of the original Christian missionaries is outlined later.

He is often represented with one or more of the following:

• A tongue of fire over his head, the flame of the Holy Spirit.

• A golden nimbus, or disc around his head, indicating his sainthood.

• A halberd, a weapon with a lance at one end and a battle-axe at the other; the weapon that killed him.

• Loaves and fishes, representing his status as an apostle.

• A book, representing the epistle he wrote.

• A long cross, the sign of his Master, Jesus.

• A club, used by the Magi priests of Persia to subdue him.

• A lance, thought by some to be the weapon of his death.

• A boat, an oar, a boat hook, an anchor, a child holding a boat... all indicating his association with the fishermen of Galilee.

• A carpenter's square, indicating his work with his cousin, Jesus, and uncle, Joseph.

• A medallion of Jesus, either in his hand or on his chest to recognize his association with the image of Edessa, believed to be the burial shroud of Jesus.

He is usually associated with the colour green, the colour of hope. Chrysoprase, a green gem of Beryl or Chalcedony, is also associated with Jude as a symbol of hope.

Jude played a vital role in the establishment of

many branches of Christianity, and so he has a number of feast days:

• In the Latin or Roman Church, the feast day of Saints Simon and Jude is October 28.

• In the Syrian calendar, because it was sometimes believed that Jude and Thaddeus were different people, St Thaddeus Day is May 14 and the Apostle Jude Day is May 19 or December 18.

• In the Ethiopian Church, his day is June 26.

• In the Egyptian church, January 26 and May 10.

• In the Coptic Church, July 2

• In the Greek Church, June 19.

• In the Armenian Church, February 16.

In 1548, Pope Paul III granted a plenary indulgence to all who visited the tomb of St Jude in Rome on his feast day, October 28. This granted the remission of punishment for all sin.

How the Legend Grew

AS A TRAINEE nurse facing daunting exams at the Newcastle Mater Hospital in Australia, Marie Scales was told: "Pray to St Jude for inspiration." Despite her fears and her lack of confidence, she did so and she succeeded beyond her dreams.

Over the years, whenever things seemed bleak and hopeless, Marie's novenas to Jude were answered. On retirement after a lifetime of nursing, she recalled the misery of a broken marriage, the ravages of ill-health and the deaths of loved ones. But in her most hopeless, desperate times, she said, Jude answered her prayers, whether they were for herself, her family or her patients.

Marie Scales always believed that, if you had

Believers flock to a St Jude Festival
in India.

Jude, you were never alone. When all else failed, Jude was always there.

Her belief is shared by millions around the world.

How did this come about?

Some say that, when Judas the Iscariot bestowed upon Jesus the saddest kiss in human history, the kiss of betrayal, the other Judas, Judas Thaddeus, was devastated. He rarely used the name "Judas" again, preferring the simple "Jude" or Thaddeus. But people were still confused between the two apostles and, for long periods of history, Jude was forgotten. Until, that is, people suffered enough to turn to the neglected apostle in desperation.

As his legend began to grow, all kinds of people petitioned his help - those in despair, the lonely, believers and doubters, Catholics, Jews, Anglicans, those without faith of any kind.

The Jesuits' *Acta Sanctorum*, in 1863, outlined lives of the saints and described devotion to Jude in some places as "amazing". The Jesuits said a booklet called *The Little Office of Jude*, published in 1826, called him "the special advocate of the unfortunate and well-nigh hopeless".

By the twentieth century, thousands of churches and shrines around the world were dedicated to him. There are said to be more churches named after Jude in the USA than anyone other than Our Lady.

Recognizing his special appeal to the terminally ill, administrators began to name hospitals and cancer treatment centres after him. His name appeared on secular activities like golf and tennis tournaments and bowling leagues. Prison chapels, including San Quentin, were dedicated to him. In Sydney, a refuge for men and a nurses' agency are named after him. These are but a few.

The Claretians, the missionary sons of the Immaculate Heart of Mary, set up the League of St Jude in 1929 to foster devotion to the apostle. In 1932, a special branch of the league was formed within the Chicago police department to place police officers under the protection of Jude.

Many other cities followed and adopted Jude as patron of their Christian, not necessarily Catholic, police organisations.

People everywhere began wearing St Jude necklaces and key-rings inscribed "St Jude Protect Me." St Jude medals are pinned on countless surgery gowns

St Jude Anglican Church,
Wexford, England.

and on those undertaking examinations.

Holy cards, with prayers and illustrations of the saint, are passed from hand to hand between loved ones.

"Look, this might sound silly, but take this... Jude helped me... he will help you."

People, even those who have no faith, take the offered medals or holy cards and tuck them away in wallet or purse... and begin to feel a faint glimmer of hope.

Jude, Hope of the Hopeless, is at work.

People of all faiths cling to one, ultimate hope - the hope of life after death. According to tradition, the famous prayer, the Apostles' Creed, was composed as a declaration of faith by the apostles after the resurrection and before they separated on their missionary journeys.

Jude's contribution? The last line: "*et vitam aeternam*" - "and life everlasting."

Jude's Missionary Journeys

JUDE PLAYED a vital, perhaps unsurpassed, role in the establishment of Christianity, despite riots, war and persecution.

After the resurrection, he was arrested in Jerusalem with the other apostles, and thrown into the dungeon, but managed to escape, with the help, according to the New Testament, of an angel. They were arrested again for preaching about Jesus, and flogged with the scourge - twenty six times on the back and thirteen on the front.

Jude was scarred for life. But the biggest scar was the scar on his soul - the shame of running away when Jesus was arrested and crucified. He resolved to devote his life to the Lord to try to erase that scar.

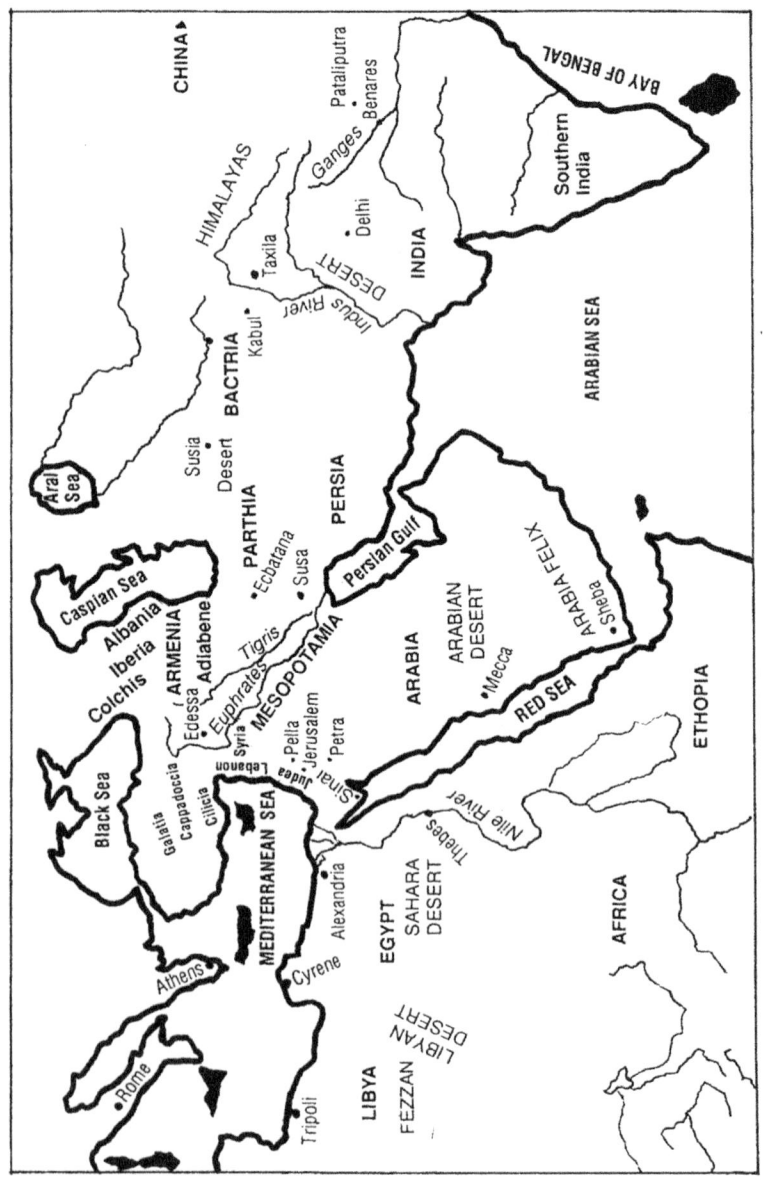

A view of the world as Jude knew it at the time of his extraordinary missionary journeys.

His journeys covered more than ten times the land distance of Saint Paul's and extended for an additional two decades. After the death of Jesus, Jude spent forty-three years "on the road", traveling more than one hundred thousand miles, by foot, donkey and camel, in doing so. By any measure, this is extraordinary.

Family Heartbreak

His mission started in AD29, when he was thirty-seven years of age, married and with children. After the descent of the Holy Spirit, as described in the New Testament, he suffered the heartbreak of leaving his family to devote his life to serving the Lord. Whenever he could, he came back to Judea to see them. His wife, Mary, came to him when she could, traveling with camel and donkey caravans. Mary also preached for him to the women cloistered behind closed doors in the custom of the times.

Jude preached in Judea, Galilee, Samaria and Lebanon, on his way to Edessa (modern-day Urfa in Southern Turkey), the capital of Osrhoene. Here he performed his first recorded miracle, curing a man called Abdus, "the second man in the kingdom", of gout. Many other healings followed.

The healing of Abgar, King of Edessa, and other healings, were described by Eusebius, the father of Christian history, in his *History of the Church,* written about 330AD.

The Famous Letters

About a year earlier, Abgar V, King of Edessa, had written to Jesus in Jerusalem, asking that he come and cure his leprosy. Jesus replied that he must complete his mission and be taken up again to his Father, but that he would send a disciple to cure the king and preach to his people. That disciple turned out to be Jude.

When Jude left home for Edessa to see the king, he took with him a priceless treasure - the burial cloth of Jesus, on which many believe the Master's image had formed.

The cloth had been removed from the empty tomb by Jude's mother, Mary, one of the women at the cross. Mary had gone to the tomb with the other women to anoint the body and prepare it properly for burial, only to find he had risen, leaving behind his burial cloth.

As Jude entered the king's audience chamber, he held the image in front of him. When Abgar saw it, he had a blinding vision, seen by no-one else, and fell to the floor. Jude knew the king had lost hope for a cure, but still touched the image to the royal feet, hands, breast and head. He laid his hands on the head of the

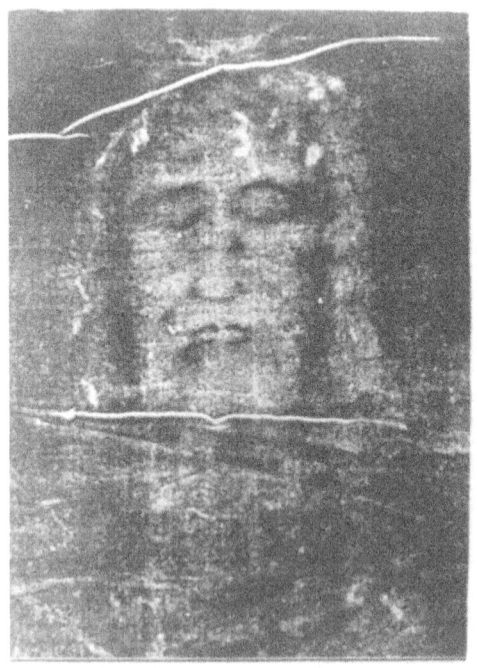

Part of the image from the Shroud of
Turin. Many believe this was the burial cloth
of Jesus, the cloth used, according to
Eusebius, to cure Abgar. This cloth, after a
long and colourful history, is now a treasure of
the Catholic Church.

leprous king - and the king was cured.

The King Was Converted

This healing turned out to be vital to the establishment and spread of Christianity. The king and many of his subjects were converted; Abgar wrote letters of introduction for Jude to other kings and leaders; and Jude, after three years of preaching in Edessa, set out with a disciple, Tobias, to preach and heal in Cilicia, Commagene, Cappadocia and Galatia.

They lived as nomads, for months and years on end, facing strange and sometimes hostile people, strange customs, strange gods. Jude struggled to overcome solitude, homesickness and despair at the enormous task in front of him.

In Cappadoccia, he worked among the victims of the flourishing slave trade - touching, healing, encouraging - and many were converted, taking the story of Jesus with them to the slave markets of the world.

Near Mount Argaeus, Jude braved wild dogs and even wilder wolves to reach people in desolated outposts.

Many, Many Gods

There were many, many gods to be overcome by the one, true God. In caves near Hattusa, Jude found sixty-three gods of the ancient Hittites. At Nemrut, he was overcome by the arrogance and the conceit of the man-made gods of Antiochus. Five years after he left Edessa, he returned, weary, lonely, depressed at the difficulties he had faced and had yet to face.

Small Christian Outposts

He had done much, and set up small Christian outposts - but it had taken its toll.

He rested in Edessa and was joined by the apostles Peter and Bartholomew. Jude wanted to take care of the flock he had established before he moved on to reach more people. He and Peter spoke to Aggai, the man who had persuaded King Abgar to contact Jesus, and anointed him Bishop of Edessa. Bishop Aggai would become a pillar of the church in the region.

The apostles commissioned Tobias to care for the believers Jude had converted to the north-west of Edessa. The flock would be well cared for.

Jude wanted to go to the north-east, to Armenia, with Bartholomew - but he was delayed by worrisome problems in Jerusalem. Jude's brother, James, had been elected Bishop of Jerusalem after the resurrection. He had faced persecution as strong leader of the

Christians. The deacon Stephen had been martyred, stoned to death, and the other James, the son of Zebedee, had been beheaded. Many believers had fled Jerusalem, but five thousand remained, facing increasing persecution. A refuge, Peter said, must be found for them.

A Plan for Refugees

Jude, Peter and Bartholomew came up with a plan to seek a refuge in Pella from King Aretas, of Arabia. With Bartholomew, he travelled to Arabia and stayed with the Arabians and Bedouin in town and tent, telling of the wonders and miracles performed by the Master and of the persecution faced by the Jerusalem assembly.

They suffered the privations of endless desert travel, faced the dangers of heat and of wild animals, including lions, and marauding bands of cut-throat Bedouin.

Finally, miracles of healing in the fortified city of Petra convinced King Aretas to allow the refugees entry to Pella, should continued persecution make it necessary.

Jude set out for Armenia with Bartholomew and a disciple called Mari. They risked their lives to talk to robbers and murderers in caves near Harput and witnessed bloodshed and savage customs in Theodosiopolis, again risking their lives to intervene.

They crossed the lower ranges of Mount Ararat, where Noah's ark had come to rest, and entered the Armenian capital of Artashat. Here Jude converted King Mithradates and members of the royal household after healing the king's crippled daughter.

Human Sacrifice

They passed through the beautiful, rugged land of the Georgians to the Black Sea, healing people of leprosy in the caves of the Ahuryan River. Jude preached in Colchis, Iberia and Caucasian Albania. In Iberia, he was sickened by the sacrifice of a human life to the goddess Selene.

They made their way back towards Judea for the Council of Jerusalem, a meeting of the apostles scheduled for AD49.

On the way, Jude was hurt in an earthquake near Mount Ararat and healed an old man of blindness at Lake Van. In Adiabene, he healed a child, the daughter of the king, and converted the royal household and many of the citizens.

Twenty years after setting out on his missionary

journeys, Jude returned to Jerusalem for the council, set up to discuss matters of doctrine, including the question of whether Gentile converts should be circumcised. Jude thought not, and soon, in the end, did the council.

Jude had returned to find his wife ill. His love for her was so deep, and he had rarely known her to be ill at all.

He was devastated when she died in his arms.

In a deep abyss of depression, Jude left Jerusalem with his brother, Simon, and walked towards Idumea and the Judean wilderness - away from where he had been preaching.

To the Point of Death

They walked almost to the point of death - down to the Dead Sea and to Mount Sinai. They trudged up to the Nile Delta, to Alexandria and other cities of Egypt. Simon tried desperately to bring Jude out of his despair.

Despite the dangers of the *khamsin*, the dreaded wind of the desert, the apostles decided to cross the deserts of Libya. Jude was still in deep depression. Finally, in the Libyan Desert, they almost died in a sandstorm.

Jude and his brother, Simon, almost perished in a fierce
sandstorm in the Libyan Desert.

Afterwards, exhausted, Jude slept and dreamt that the Lord was calling him again. He had been called by Jesus. He had been called by the Holy Spirit. Now he was called again. In the morning, his spirits soared and life flooded back. He vowed he would never again allow despair to triumph over hope.

Preaching with Joy

With great joy, he preached with Simon throughout Libya and Egypt.

However, in the midst of their jubilation, a letter arrived from their brother, James, Bishop of Jerusalem.

Their father, Cleophas, had died, killed on the steps of the Temple defending James and the name of the Master, Jesus. In Edessa, King Abgar had also died after a long reign, and his son Ma'nu V was on the throne. In Armenia, there was a build-up towards war between Parthia and Rome, with tension high among Armenian Christians, who were caught in the middle.

The apostles returned to Jerusalem, where Simon stayed to help James, while Jude left to preach in India with Bartholomew.

Gateway to India

Jude crossed savage mountain passes to Taxila,

the gateway to India, and was overwhelmed by his first taste of the noise and confusion of India. They dropped down into the furnace of the Great Indian Desert and preached in villages between the Indus River and Delhi. The monsoon came roaring in on howling winds, with stunning effects on India and its people. Jude sought out the poor, the people hit hardest by flood and mud.

Sages of Three Faiths

He followed the path trod by the sages of three faiths - Hinduism, Buddhism and Jainism. He was overwhelmed by the many gods, by the chanting in ancient temples, by the deep spirituality of the people. He survived a confrontation with a tiger and was welcomed as a sadhu, a holy man, wherever he went.

In the holy city of Benares he found his most eager listeners were the poor, the outcasts, the people who could look forward to little except misery. They clung to his message of hope.

Jude visited King Kadphises in Pataliputra and found him anxious about a possible war with the Parthians or China. The king showed Jude the strength of his War Elephant Army and urged him to tell the Parthians, in the hope of averting war.

Jude faced troubles in all directions.

Persecution

In Edessa, Christians were being persecuted. King Ma'nu V died after a short reign and Abgar's second son took the throne as Ma'nu VI. He was hostile to the Christians and killed Bishop Aggai in front of the stunned believers. The Christians hid the burial shroud of Jesus within the western gate to the city, where it would be safe, but could still protect Edessa.

In Jerusalem, the Romans and the Jewish High Priest were persecuting the Christians. Nero was Emperor of Rome and slaughtering Christians by the thousand.

A King is Murdered

In Armenia, King Mithradates was murdered and, soon after, the Parthian, King Vologases, overran Armenia and installed his brother, Tiridates, on the throne. This incensed Nero, who sent his legions to recapture Armenia and install a Roman king. The Christians lived in constant terror and feared more reprisals from Parthia.

By now, AD62, Jude was seventy years of age and weary. He returned to Jerusalem just as his brother James was thrown from a parapet of the Temple by

Jude had intended to write a major work for the new Church believers, but ran out of time.

Instead, he wrote the epistle that bears his name and now forms part of the New Testament.

an angry mob incited by the High Priest. The Bishop of Jerusalem was then stoned and finally killed with a blow from a club.

More than five thousand Christians fled the persecution in Jerusalem and streamed towards the refuge Jude had set up in Pella, Arabia. There Jude rested and saw the community established in its new home. Simon was elected Bishop of Jerusalem to replace James, though he might never set foot in David's City again.

Jude's Epistle

Bartholomew left to comfort believers in war-torn Armenia, while Jude and Simon trained young deacons and began to send them out to the church communities everywhere. Jude wrote his epistle at Pella, warning Christians of false teachers who had wormed their way into their midst.

He grew restless and set out for Mesopotamia and Persia, both controlled by the Parthians, with Simon and a disciple, Craton. Though several years had passed, Jude was still tormented by the threat of war between Parthia and India. And he still felt the scar on his soul and the obsession to serve the Lord.

At Hatra, in Mesopotamia, Jude rescued a poor

woman who had been sentenced to death by the priests for adultery.

This incurred the wrath of two Magi priests, Zaroes and Arfaxat, and set them on a long collision course with the apostle.

The Magi had been praying for rain without success and now challenged Jude, if his God was so powerful, to end the drought. Jude prayed and, immediately afterwards, the eternal flame of the god Shamash - kept alight always in his honour - went out. The next morning, rain fell to end the drought. The Magi were furious, but the crowds flocked to hear Jude preach.

Inspired Words

The apostles set off to journey down the Euphrates River in Mesopotamia. Jude laid his hands on a demented man and prayed, and the demon left him. A large crowd came to the river to hear Jude. He spoke such inspired words about the Holy Spirit that hundreds surged forward to be baptized in the waters of the Euphrates.

In Babylon, Jude clashed with people set in their ways when he told stories from the Book of Daniel, which was set in Babylon. People attacked him for criticizing the gods of Babylon and the crowd became

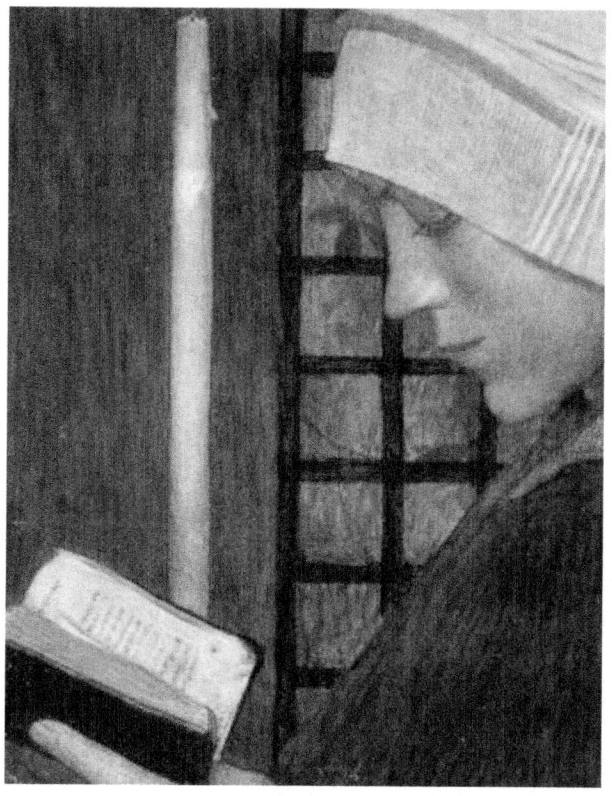

Wherever Jude travelled, people came closer to
God. And, in the years since, Jude has
become the intermediary between the outcasts of
the world and the Almighty.

angry. Jude stormed among them condemning their gods of gold and stone and challenging these gods to strike him down if they had any power.

Jude's reputation as a holy man grew and many followed him. He grew weary, but persevered, drawing himself, and those whose lives he touched, closer to God.

While this was happening, war continued in Armenia. Bartholomew went to the Georgians during a lull in the fighting and, after expelling a demon from a king's daughter, was set upon by the king's brother, who shared the throne, and was flogged to death in the town of Albanopolis, by the Caspian Sea.

Towers of Silence

At Ecbatana, in Parthian territory, Jude witnessed a bull slaughtered as a sacrifice to the gods, and a naked young initiate washed in the bull's blood. The apostle reeled away from the barbarism and left the city through what he discovered was the gate of the *dakhmas*, the towers of silence.

These were raised platforms, on which kites and vultures were feeding. This was the "funeral of the desert". The Magi did not allow cremation because this would contaminate the fire, which was sacred. Bodies of the dead were left on the platforms to be eaten by hyenas and other animals, and picked at by the birds. The stench was nauseating.

Jude reeled away again, only to find himself among men undergoing *askesis*, a "taming of the flesh". Because they thought it brought them close to the gods, men mutilated themselves, scourged themselves, starved themselves. Some died of the torture they inflicted on themselves. Masses of flies swarmed over the mutilations. Men wallowed in their own waste.

Jude swayed on his feet. He had no words. He touched a man. Then another. He touched, held, laid his hands on them until he could no longer see and Craton led him away.

At the city gates, they looked back. Men were talking, holding the place where had touched them. Some were rising ... and looking towards the city.

Wonders of Persia

When the Magi, Zaroes and Arfaxat, arrived in Ecbatana, the apostles left, rather than stir up trouble for the believers. They saw the wonders of Persia and preached to the poor and the downtrodden in isolated villages.

In Susa, they crossed paths with the Magi again. They watched as Zaroes and Arfaxat and a priest magician, the MashMashu, tried to exorcise a demon from a man who had paid a fee to the temple for the service. The MashMashu had performed an elaborate ritual for three days, but, in the end, it failed - and the man collapsed in convulsions.

After a clash with the Magi - Jude came forward and healed the man.

The Magi were now hostile and stirred up hatred of the apostles wherever they went. Despite this, they were still baptizing new Christians, who now numbered in the tens of thousands in Mesopotamia and Persia. However, as they entered the temple city of Dur Untashi, they were set upon with clubs by men sent by the Magi, and severely beaten.

When they were able, the apostles pressed on to Persepolis, where, after a period of recuperation, they went to the square to preach. While they were there, Craton rushed to them with a letter from Judah, Jude's son.

The Fall of Jerusalem

Jerusalem had fallen to the Romans. More than a million Jews had starved or been put to the sword.

Not a stone was left upon a stone. A hundred thousand of the young had been pressed into slavery and prostitution.

While the old apostles wept, Craton realized that the Magi had sealed off the square and the people had left.

The square was now ominously quiet. A sacred bull was released into the square. Large, yellow, bleeding. It had been hurt and was terrified. It pawed the ground and charged at Jude. At the last moment, it veered away and lunged in a fury at the entrance to the square, and at the Magi who were hiding behind it. The bull, representing the warrior god, Verethragna, had turned on his own priests.

Simon returned to Pella to comfort those who had lost loved ones in Jerusalem, while Jude set out to find the Parthian Army in Bactria, which was a part of Parthian territory and within striking distance of India. Jude was determined to see if the threat of war still existed before he returned home to end his missionary life. He had promised King Kadphises, of India, to do what he could to avert war. He saw it as his last mission.

He found the army and its Commander-in-chief, Prince Verardach, near Herat, in Bactria. They were, indeed, battle-ready. The prince had already heard of Jude. The Magi had reached him first.

Jude told him of the massive Indian army he had seen at Pataliputra, and of the frightening war elephants.

Ready for War

While Verardach was weighing up his options, Jude sent Craton to India on horseback to talk to King Kadphises and return in all haste. The Parthians were ready for war and Jude was distraught at the thought of bloodshed, yet he knew both sides would avoid war if they could.

Jude was called back to Verardach's tent and found idols standing on pedestals at the entrance. The Magi were there.

Zaroes said he had brought the gods to help the commander, but Jude ridiculed them. Zaroes said the war would be terrible and the war elephants of India would run amok. The war would be long, he said. Jude again condemned the gods as useless if they could not prevent war. As he spoke, a gust of wind toppled the idols from their pedestals and smashed them, sparking another clash with the Magi. Verardach asked Jude about the war and the apostle asked for time to consult God. He was desperately awaiting the return of Craton from India. The commander gave Jude one day - "then I march on India".

Jude spent a sleepless night of prayer, but in the morning, Craton returned. "The Indians... they are coming!" he said.

The apostle went to Verardach and found him stirred to war by the Magi. He told the commander that ambassadors from India would arrive the next day to negotiate for peace.

"Your gods lie," he said. "Your war will be over before it starts."

The ambassadors arrived and peace was declared.

Verardach ordered that the Magi be burned alive as punishment for their false prophecy, but Jude intervened and their lives were spared.

Incited to Anger

Verardach invited Jude and Craton to a feast with Vologases, King of Parthia. When they arrived at the king's tent, they found the Magi had arrived first and incited the King to anger over Jude's treatment of the gods. The Magi released the Evil One, Ahriman, in the form of two snakes and ordered Jude and Craton to pick them up.

"If your God is powerful, they will not harm

Craton was taking Jude home, after 43 years on the road as a missionary. Jude was exhausted and his work was done. They made it to Susia, on the edge of the Sand Desert.

you," they said.

Jude remembered a snake charmer in India and showed Craton how to pick up a snake. They put the snakes under their mantles, fearful that they would strike, but they did not. They put the snakes on the ground again and ordered the Magi to pick them up - and the snakes struck. Jude quickly removed the snakes from the Magi. He laid his hands on the priests and prayed that they would recover from the snake bites.

Going home at last

For Jude, it was all over. His work was done. He had averted war. At last he was going home. He was eighty. His work as a missionary was over after forty three years. He was spent.

He stopped with Craton at a town called Susia and was shocked to be confronted again by Zaroes and Arfaxat, who had prepared a trap. Rough hands dragged Jude through the sand to the temple steps. The Magi began to stir up the crowd with angry words about Jude's treatment of the gods. Seventy priests, all with clubs, lined the temple steps. The crowd screamed: "Death!", but Zaroes tried for one last victory.

"If you bow down in worship of Mithra," he said, "we will spare your life." The ultimate challenge. Jude refused, and the priests began to batter the old man with their clubs.

Craton was stunned. He could not believe they would do this to an old man, a holy man. But eyes and ears will not be deceived. Sights and sounds of barbarism will not be denied.

An Unholy Place

In the temple court, in this unholy place, a thousand white-robed men jostled in anticipation, while here and there a shameless woman in black watched out of veiled eyes. They listened in silence as the death sentence was pronounced and murmured as the executioner appeared.

Craton watched helplessly, held by guards, as Jude rose in a daze to his knees. He saw the holy man rock slightly, a smile somehow showing, a radiance. "I think I hear the Lord calling me." The words whispered out of a parched throat and bloodied face as the executioner brandished the halberd, the combined lance and battle-axe.

The Magi nodded to the executioner, who plunged the lance, suddenly, into the base of the holy one's spine. He achieved his purpose.

The condemned man's head lifted off the sand, his back arched, his neck became exposed.

The halberd twirled, the battle-axe swooped in a fierce arch... but Jude's soul, surely cleansed of its scar of shame, was already on its way home to the Lord.

The Halberd

The Abgar/Jesus Letters

JESUS WAS a man of the spoken word. He was not a writer, but there is a record of one letter he wrote. It was his reply to a request for help from King Abgar, of Edessa.

The letter was recorded in many places, but was first mentioned by Christianity's "Father of Ecclesiastical History", Eusebius, in *The History of the Church*, written about AD330. Eusebius said he translated the letters himself from the Syriac, when he found them in the Record Office at Edessa.

In AD383, a pilgrim-nun, Egeria, visited Edessa accompanied by the Bishop of Edessa, Eulogios. She recorded in her diary that she had seen the letters in the archives. They were still recorded as being in Edessa in AD544.

The letters are believed to be among documents found in the Nitrian monastery in the desert of Lower Egypt between 1841 and 1847 - and now kept in the British Museum.

In AD494, Pope Gelasius listed documents to be included in the canon of the Catholic Church, but the Abgar/Jesus letters were not among them. Despite this, their fame spread around the world. They were included in the Syrian liturgy and copies became well known in places as far away as Spain, Italy and Ireland. Versions appeared in Norse, Danish and Anglo-Saxon.

In the nineteenth century, framed copies were hung over doorways in Shropshire, England, and other places to protect the occupants, in much the same way as the people of Edessa used them almost two thousand years earlier.

A Holy Charm

People are still known to wear copies as a holy charm "to protect against lightning and hail, and perils by sea and by land, by day and by night, and in dark places."

In India, in the nineteenth century, printed copies of the Edessa letters were discovered by an English writer. People wore them as protection against fever and other maladies.

The letters were also inscribed in stone in Greek text in the Forty Caves area of Edessa. A photograph, taken in 1952-55, appeared in J.B. Segal's *Edessa: The Blessed City.*

The original letter by King Abgar in Edessa was taken by "the swiftest courier in the kingdom", Ananias, to Jesus in Jerusalem. Here is the text of the letter:

ABGAR Uchama, King of Edessa, to Jesus, the gracious saviour who has appeared in the Jerusalem region, greetings.

I have heard reports about you and about the cures you perform without medicine and without herbs. It is said that you can make the blind see and the lame walk, that you cleanse lepers, cast out impure spirits and demons, that you can heal those suffering lingering, painful diseases, and raise the dead.

And when I heard these things about you, I concluded that one of two things must be true: either you are God and came down from heaven to do these things, or else you who do these things are the Son of God. I am therefore writing to you to beg that you take the trouble to come to me and heal the disease from which I suffer.

I have also heard that the Jews are murmuring against you and plotting to injure you. My city is very small, but much esteemed, and it is big enough for both of us.

The reply by Jesus was as follows:

JESUS to the Toparch Abgar, King of Edessa, by the messenger Ananias, greetings.

Blessed are you who have believed in me without having seen me. For it is written that those who have seen me will not believe in me, and that those who have not seen me will believe and be saved.

But, in regard to your request that I should come to you, it is necessary for me to complete all that I was sent here to do, and, after completing these things, I must be taken up again to him who sent me.

After I have been taken up, I will send you one of my disciples to heal your disease and bring life to you and those with you.

The disciple sent to heal Abgar's leprosy and to preach to the people of Edessa was Jude.

The Image of Edessa

MANY PEOPLE around the world believe the image taken by Jude to Edessa and used to cure King Abgar is the same cloth now known as the Shroud of Turin.

Even Pope John Paul II declared his belief that the shroud was an authentic relic on April 28, 1989 - a year after the controversial carbon-dating tests that declared it a fake and dated it between 1260 and 1390. Since then, some experts believe the evidence has been overwhelming that those tests were flawed.

A British author now resident in Australia, Ian Wilson, has assembled the most detailed evidence that the image of Edessa is the Shroud of Turin. His study has extended for more than two decades and is recorded in several books, including his latest, *The Blood and the Shroud,* in 1997. Other writers and scientists have also supported the idea and details can be found on the Internet.

The possible journey of the image from Edessa to Turin and the present day is given by Ian Wilson in several of his books, but here we will simply relate the story of the image up to the stage where conjecture starts.

The discovery of the image in Edessa is described in a fanciful way, as was common at the time, but this need not detract from the essential facts of the story.

Siege of Edessa

According to the Syrian-born historian, Evagrius, the Persian king, Chosroes Nirhivan, laid siege to Edessa in AD544. When the aggressor had almost succeeded in scaling the citadel mount by night and all seemed lost, the Bishop had a vision that told him where to find the image.

He found it in the western Kappe Gate, where Bishop Palut, Aggai's successor, had hidden it for protection in AD57. It was sealed up with a red tile, also imprinted with an image of Jesus, and known to have been made on the instructions of King Abgar.

With the tile and the image was a candle "still

burning after 500 years". The defenders sprinkled the cloth with water and shook it at the Persian siege works, "which were immediately consumed by fire". The image had saved the city.

The cloth was kept in the Hagia Sophia of Edessa, built after the disastrous flood of AD525. Time after time, enemies threatened Edessa unless the people surrendered the relic - but Edessans, both Christian and Muslim, refused to part with it.

Early in the ninth century, three Eastern Christian Melchite patriarchs listed icons for the emperor, Theophilus. The image of Edessa was the first item on the list.

Pieces of Silver

In AD944, with a powerful Christian Byzantine enemy at the gates, the Mohammedan ruler of Edessa found himself under pressure from the Muslim caliph in Baghdad, who forced him to trade the image. In return for the image, the emperor, Romanus Lecapenus, released many Muslims from Byzantine prisons and handed the Edessan ruler a fortune of twelve thousand pieces of silver. He also promised Edessa freedom from any future attack.

As Christians took the image to Constantinople,

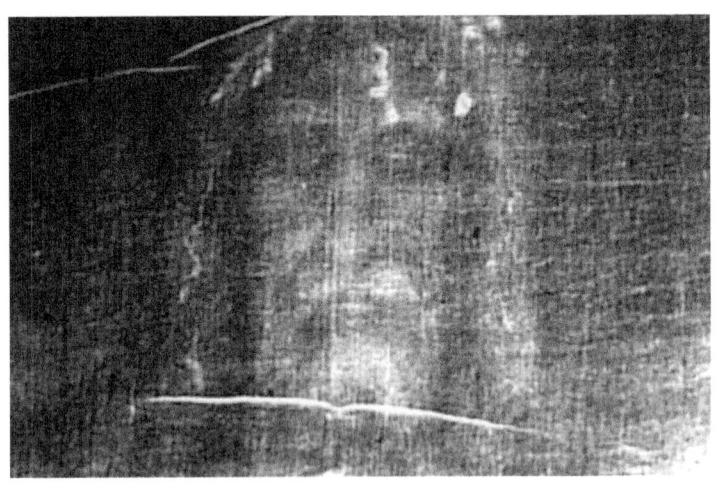

Since about 1150AD, the great artists of the world have used the image of Edessa as the base model to depict the face of Jesus Christ.

a great storm lashed Edessa. It was the beginning of the end for the city that had believed itself protected for centuries by the image. There were Byzantine invasions, despite the promise of immunity, attacks by Muslim warlords and even a famine to send Edessa into a decline from which it has never recovered.

The image was secured in the Hagia Sophia of Constantinople in AD944 "for the glory of the faithful, for the safety of the emperors, for the preservation of the entire city and the way of life of the Christian empire".

Image Carried in Procession

The image was carried in procession in 1036, during the reign of Michael Paphlagos, and again in 1058, when Christian Arab writer Abu Nasr Yahya recorded seeing it in the Hagia Sophia, Constantinople.

Earlier, the *Acta Thaddaei*, a sixth century text, described the cloth as being "doubled in four" - the first such mention and one of the clues to link the image with the Shroud of Turin.

Around AD757, Pope Stephen III described it as the cloth bearing the image of "the whole body of the Lord". This was the first reference to the "Mandylion" image being of a whole body. The same statement was made in the twelfth century by an English monk, Ordericus Vitalis, and by a Vatican library codex, and, in the thirteenth century, by Gervase of Tilbury.

The Face of Christ

From the twelfth century, artists represented the face of Christ as depicted on the image of Edessa - identical to what became known as the Shroud of Turin.

In 1201, a Greek, Nicholas Mesarites, described the cloth as "wrapping the mysterious, naked dead body after the passion" - the first such reference. In 1203, French soldier Robert de Clari described the image in Constantinople as "the sydoine in which our Lord had been wrapped".

One year later, in 1204, Constantinople was sacked by the Fourth Crusade, when Christian fought Christian, and the image of Edessa disappeared.

The cloth known as the Shroud of Turin surfaced in France in 1353, in the possession of Geoffrey de Charny. From there on, the Shroud is well documented by other writers and historians.

For those who believe the two cloths are one and the same, the one hundred and fifty years between the disappearance of the image of Edessa and the fresh emergence of the Shroud of Turin is the difficulty.

Believers think the image was taken from Constantinople by the French, who were there during the Fourth Crusade. The French Knights Templar provided much of the finance for the Fourth Crusade and acted as guardians of relics taken during the crusade. It was a time of flourishing trade in relics.

The Knights Templar had secret rites at the beginning of the fourteenth century, involving a strange object - a mysterious "head" they worshiped, "a bearded head, which they adored, kissed and called their Saviour".

Arrested and Tortured

In 1307, all Templars were arrested by the King of France, Philip the Fair, and subjected to the tortures of the Inquisition, during which they confessed to having the "head".

Geoffrey de Charney, a leader of the Templars, was burned at the stake in 1314. Geoffrey de Charny, the first known owner of the Shroud in the west, began appearing in French military records in 1337 and lived until 1356. The two men were a generation apart. Was there a family link?

Believe what you will - if the image of Edessa is

the Shroud of Turin, it survived at least five floods (up to AD668), an earthquake (AD678), danger from marauding bands in France (1418), a fire (1532), in which the Shroud was damaged, an invasion of Savoy by French troops (1535), a plague (1630), air raids in the First World War (1918), an arson attempt (1972) and another fire (1997).

Impossible? Ah, but is not Jude the Saint of the Impossible?

For many believers, the burial cloth of Jesus, rescued from the tomb by Jude's mother, taken to Edessa by Jude, used to cure King Abgar of leprosy, held as a protective talisman for Edessa and surviving all manner of catastrophe in the years since, is one of the most hallowed treasures on earth.

It would be a great comfort and inspiration to believers if the image of Edessa, the burial cloth of Jesus, had survived those two thousand years. But, if it did not, devotion to Jude and his Master will not be diminished.

The Epistle of Jude

JUDE WROTE his epistle with a reed pen on papyrus. The year was AD64 and the place was Pella, to the east of Jerusalem, in Arabia. Five thousand Christians had fled the Holy City after the martyrdom of Jude's brother, James.

Jude had begun work on a larger book to serve as a summary of the faith after he was gone, but that work was never completed. He still had missionary work to do in Mesopotamia and Persia, and an urgent problem of false teachers had arisen in communities of Jewish Christians.

These men were attending the agapés, the feasts of love, the forerunners of the Mass and Christian service, and they were telling Christians they could sin with impunity because they would be saved by God's grace.

Jude felt he had to respond immediately to this challenge with a trumpet call to Christians to defend the faith. Unless these impostors were removed, the very existence of the Christian communities was under threat.

He had given thirty five years of his life to creating these communities after the Master's death. He was not getting any younger - he was now seventy two years of age - but he would fight evil and deception wherever he found it, and he would fight it with vigour.

He cast his mind over past stories of such deceit and wrote in terms his believers of Jewish background would understand. His indignation blazed as he spoke of the evil teachers, but his tone softened as he addressed his beloved Christians. This is the text of the only writing credited to Jude:

FROM Jude, servant of Jesus Christ and brother of James, to those who are called, to those who are dear to God the Father and kept safe for Jesus Christ, wishing you all mercy and peace and love.

My dear friends, at a time when I was eagerly looking forward to writing to you about the salvation that we all share, I have been forced to write to you now and appeal to you to fight hard for the faith, which has been once and for all entrusted to the saints. Certain people have infiltrated among you, and they are the ones you had a warning about, in writing, long ago, when they were condemned for denying all religion, turning the grace of our God into immorality, and rejecting our only Master and Lord, Jesus Christ.

I should like to remind you - though you have already learnt it once and for all - how the Lord rescued the nation from Egypt, but afterwards he still destroyed the men who did not trust him.

Next, let me remind you of the angels who had supreme authority, but did not keep it and left their appointed sphere; he has kept them down in the dark, in spiritual

THE GENERAL EPISTLE of JUDE

Salutation

JUDE,ᵃ the servant of Jesus Christ, and brother of James,

To them that are sanctified by God the Father, and preserved in Jesus Christ, and called:

2 Mercy unto you, and peace, and love, be multiplied.

Judgment on False Teachers

(2 Pet. 2:1-17)

3 Beloved, when I gave all diligence to write unto you of the common salvation, it was needful for me to write unto you, and exhort *you* that ye should earnestly contend for the faith which was once delivered unto the saints. 4 For there are certain men crept in unawares, who were before of old ordained to this condemnation, ungodly men, turning the grace of our God into lasciviousness, and denying the only Lord God, and * our Lord Jesus Christ.

5 I will therefore put you in remembrance, this, how

Moses, durs not railing accusation, rebuke thee, in those things whic what they know no in those things th 11 Woe unto the the way of Cain, the error of Ba perished in the 12 These are spo ity, when they themselves wit without water trees whose fr twice dead, 13 raging way their own sh whom is rese ness for ever 14 And E Adam, prof hold, the L of his saints all, and to among the which they

The Epistle of Jude in the new testament.

chains, to be judged on the great day. The fornication of Sodom and Gomorrah and the other nearby towns was equally unnatural, and it is a warning to us that they are paying for their crimes in eternal fire.

Nevertheless, these people are doing the same: in their delusions, they not only defile their own bodies and disregard authority, but abuse the glorious angels as well.

Not even the archangel Michael, when he was engaged in argument with the devil about the corpse of Moses, dared to denounce him in the language of abuse; all he said was, "Let the Lord correct you." But these people abuse anything they do not understand; and the only things they do understand - just by nature, like unreasoning animals - will turn out to be fatal to them.

May they get what they deserve, because they have followed Cain; they have rushed to make the same mistake as Balaam and for the same reward; they have rebelled just as Korah did - and share the same fate.

They are a dangerous obstacle to your community meals, coming for the food and quite shamelessly only looking after themselves. They are like clouds blown about by the winds and bringing no rain, or like barren trees, which are then uprooted in the winter and so are twice dead; like wild sea waves capped with shame as if with foam; or like *shooting stars bound for an eternity of black darkness.*

It was with them in mind that Enoch, the seventh patriarch from Adam, made his prophecy when he said, "I tell you, the Lord will come with his saints in their tens of thousands, to pronounce judgment on all mankind and to sentence the wicked for all the wicked things they have done, and for all the defiant things said against him by irreligious sinners."

They are mischief-makers, grumblers governed only by their own desires, with mouths full of boastful talk, ready with flattery for other people when they see some advantage in it.

But remember, my dear friends, what the apostles of our Lord Jesus Christ told you to expect. "At the end of time," they told you, "there are going to be people who will sneer at religion and follow nothing but their own desires for wickedness."

These unspiritual and selfish people are nothing but mischief-makers.

But you, my dear friends, must use your most holy faith as your foundation and build on that, praying in the Holy Spirit; keep yourselves within the love of God and wait for the mercy of our Lord Jesus Christ to give you eternal life.

When there are some who have doubts, reassure them; when there are some to be saved from the fire, pull them out; but there are others to whom you must be kind with great caution, keeping your distance even from outside clothes, which is contaminated by vice.

Glory be to him who can keep you from falling and bring you, safe to his glorious presence, innocent and happy. To God, the only God, who saves us through Jesus Christ our Lord, be the glory, majesty, authority and power, which he had before time began, now and forever.

Amen.

The Question Jude Asked

AS AN ACTIVE participant in his family's olive oil business, Jude had seen much more of the world than most of his fellow apostles. He was convinced of a simple truth: God loved everyone - not just the chosen people, the Jews.

He had great difficulty reconciling a Jewish law that said foreigners, Gentiles, were unclean - a law that resulted in separation, heartbreak, death - with a law that said: "Love them as you love yourselves."

And that was why the words of Jesus Christ

came as a burst of sunlight to the apostle. It was one thing, as Jews, to think you were the people chosen by God to receive his love directly; it was another to exclude all other people from that love.

At the Last Supper, Jude could not hold back the question: "Lord, how is it that you will reveal yourself to us and not to the world?"

The answer from Jesus contained some of the most beautiful words in the Gospel of John.

"Whoever loves me will obey my teaching. My Father will love him and my Father and I will come to him and live with him...

"The helper, the Holy Spirit, whom the Father will send in my name, will teach you everything and make you remember everything I have told you...

"Peace is what I leave with you; it is my own peace that I give you. Do not be worried or upset; do not be afraid. You have heard me say to you: I am leaving, but I will come back to you. If you love me, you will be glad I am going to the Father, for he is greater than I.

"If you remain in me and my words remain in you, then you will ask for anything you wish and you shall have it. I love you just as the Father loves me. Remain in my love...

"I have told you this so that my joy may be in you and so that your joy may be complete...

"My commandment is this: Love one another, just as I love you. The greatest love you can have for your friends is to give your life for them.

"I call you my friends. You did not choose me, I chose you and appointed you to go and bear much fruit, the kind of fruit that endures."

And after he died, he appeared to the apostles and spoke the words Jude sorely wanted to hear:

"Go to all peoples everywhere and make them my disciples. And I will be with you always, even to the end of the world."

And that became Jude's mission.

Jude's relics

THE DISCIPLE Craton gathered up the body of the holy one from the bloodied sand of Susia. He cleaned it and anointed it with the olive oil Jude loved and with spices and fragrances. He wrapped it in much linen and placed it reverently in a wooden box, placed the box on the tray of a cart and made the fifteen hundred mile journey home to Pella.

There was great lamenting and the grief spread to many villages, many cities, many countries.

King Abgar, of Edessa, had requested that he and Jude be buried together, and Simon and Judah honoured that request. And so Judas Thaddeus was laid

One of the many Saint Jude shrines in America and around the world. Shrines have multiplied since the first shrine at Edessa in line with the growth of the faithful who believe in this saint and petition him.

to rest in the palace square in Edessa, and later his remains and those of the king were moved to an ornate tomb outside the city walls.

Christians in Edessa, under threat from advancing Parthians, moved Jude's body to the Church of St John the Baptist in Edessa - and this church became the first shrine to honour the saint.

Stone Sarcophagus

His remains - his relics - were later transferred to St Peter's Basilica in Rome, where they now rest behind a grill in an ancient stone sarcophagus. In AD800, some were sent by Pope Leo III to Charlemagne, who received them on Christmas Day after his coronation as ruler of the Holy Roman Empire. These relics were deposited in and remain in Toulouse, France.

From this time, special Mass prayers in honour of Simon and Jude began appearing in France, Germany and Italy.

The conversion of whole nations to Christianity created a new demand for relics. Soon prayers were being offered to Jude throughout western Europe and his relics began to spread, like the flame of hope, to many countries of the world.

Relics found their way to Cologne, to the Church of St Mary in Capitolio, to a Benedictine abbey in Prussia, to Australia, to hundreds of Jude shrines around the world.

In 1994, Pope John Paul II sent relics of Jude and Bartholomew, the First Illuminators of Armenia, to Vasken I, Catholicos of the Armenian Apostolic Church - together with a prayer for reunion of the churches.

The flame still burns

The poor, the sick, the troubled have no hope of obtaining a relic for themselves, though they visit shrines in their millions. But they do the next best thing. They carry Jude medals, holy cards, necklaces, key-rings - anything to focus their attention on the saint and on their petitions to him.

They pray before his statue. They keep copies of the Abgar/Jesus letters as holy charms and they anoint the sick with blessed olive oil - Jude Oil.

In this way, though they may feel distant from God, they draw close to one who is close to the Almighty - and so they draw close to God.

Jude's Family

LITTLE IS known of Mary of Cleophas, Jude's mother, after the death of Jesus, but it is believed she passed her years in the company of her cousin, Mary, mother of Jesus.

Tradition has it that she sailed to the south of France with Lazarus, his sisters Martha and Mary, Salome and Mary.

There, the memory is still venerated.

Jude's younger brother, Joseph, and his sisters, Melkha and Eskha, and his daughters are thought to have lived and died in Pella. Joseph became an elder of the Pella community. Jude's son, Judah, became the third Bishop of Jerusalem, and Simon, son of Simon, became the fourth bishop.

The emperor Domitian (AD81-96) ordered the execution of all who were of David's line, both Jews and Christians.

Towards the end of his reign, Domitian had Jude's grandsons, Zoker and James, brought before him. Someone had informed against them.

They admitted they were of David's line. When Domitian asked what property and money they had, Zoker and James said they had only nine thousand denarii between them, not in money, but in the value of thirty nine plethra of land, from which they raised taxes by their own toil.

They showed the emperor their calloused hands as evidence.

Not of This World

When asked about Christ and his kingdom, they said it was not of this world, but in heaven, and would be established at the end of the world.

Domitian found no fault with them and released them.

Others who had been banished also returned to their homes, including the apostle John, who, after exile on the isle of Patmos, returned to live at Ephesus.

The two grandsons became leaders of the church and lived to the time of the Emperor Trajan (AD98-117).

Another who lived to Trajan's time was Simon, Jude's brother and Bishop of Jerusalem. According to historian Hegesippus, Simon was martyred at the age of one hundred and twenty. This seems extraordinary, but he would have been this age if he lived to the time of Trajan. He was subjected to a variety of tortures for days on end and then, after amazing his judge and assessors with his endurance, the old man was finally crucified.

In the footsteps of Jude, the other apostles and Jude's family, came men and women to keep the flame of hope alive. Many of them died for their trouble, because the persecutions continued. There were periods of rest, when Christians enjoyed the peace of their beliefs, but then the bloodletting would start again. The flame would flicker, but always it would flare again.

The Spread of the Churches

AFTER JUDE, the churches he had founded passed into new hands. The dedication and faith of these believers unleashed a powerful new force in the Mediterranean world and beyond. More resilient than opposing forces, the Christian religion, as preached by Jude and the apostles, endured through the persecution of a succession of rulers.

It was a faith that brought compassion and dignity to the disheartened, the sick, the bereaved - and it gave them hope of endless happiness beyond the grave - *et vitam aeternum*. It offered so much and demanded so little - and so it spread.

The first specially built place of worship in Christian history was built in Edessa. Both Osrhoene, with its capital of Edessa, and Armenia have both claimed to be the first Christian nation. It is generally accepted that Edessa became the first Christian city, in AD300, and Armenia the first Christian country a year later.

By the fifth century, Edessa was a major centre of Christianity, with as many as three hundred churches and monasteries. Pilgrims came vast distances to seek relics of Jude. Thousands of hermits and monks lived in its caves, leading an extraordinary life of prayer and shunning bread, meat and wine.

In AD299, a Christian called Gregory was thrown into prison by Armenia's king, Tiridates III. Within two years, according to legend, demons invaded the king and turned him into a pig. Heartbroken by his torment, the king's sister begged Gregory to help, and he promptly cast out the demons in God's name. Cured, Tiridates declared Armenia the first Christian kingdom in AD301.

St Gregory thus became the Second Illuminator of Armenia, after St Jude and St Bartholomew.

Children as Martyrs

Georgia became Christian when St Nino convinced Iberia to follow Armenia about nine years later. The Iberian ruling class adopted Christianity well, but, at a place called Kola, in south-western Georgia, parents hurled their children into a pit and stoned them to death, rather than submit to conversion. These children are numbered among the martyrs of the Georgian church.

The Georgians and the Armenians became outposts of Christianity to the east, as did Lebanon to the west.

Twelve years after Armenia converted to Christianity, the Emperor Constantine's Edict of Milan declared tolerance of Christians throughout the Roman Empire.

In Adiabene, Christianity survived and flourished among the Assyrian peoples. Jude was the first Patriarch of the Assyrian Church of the East. This church spread from Arbela, where Jude had healed the king's daughter, to surrounding areas of Syria, Persia and Mesopotamia. It became the largest church in the world by the twelfth century, extending from Syria to China, Korea, Japan and the Philippines.

Where it all Started

It was overwhelmed by the Mogul Timurlane and is now a small church in northern Iraq - where it all started with Jude. Bartholomew, Mari and St

The Christian Church, as established by Jude and the apostles
and disciples, spread to the four corners of the earth. This is
the Saint Jude Chapel in Manila.

Thomas are also listed as early patriarchs. Today's Assyrians number about three million people, who belong to three churches.

The church spread along all the roads travelled by Jude. It followed rivers and trade routes to Dura, Seleucia and Ctesiphon in Mesopotamia; south through Bostra and Petra into Arabia; westward into the far reaches of Egypt and Libya, and through Egypt into Africa. The faith travelled the Old Silk Road through the land of the Parthians to China, with bishops along the way at Samarkand and Kashgar. India looked to the archbishop in Iraq as their leader, with Christian communities in the north and also in the south, where St Thomas preached. Even in China and India, prayers were said in Syriac, the language of Edessa.

By the year AD300, one quarter of the population in the east were Christian, and one twentieth in the west.

The religion founded by the carpenter from Nazareth and preached by an olive grove worker from Judea dominated the Roman Empire by the fourth century and began to spread the flame of hope to the four corners of the world. Nothing else, before or since, has had such an effect on the history and civilization of the world.

Footnote

As this book was going to press in 2014, the small church in the north of Iraq was overrun by militant Muslims trying to set up a new Muslim state across northern Iraq and parts of Syria.

According to news reports, the town of Mosul had been home to 60,000 Christians. This had been reduced to 35,000 because of recent violence.

At this time, however, the entire 35,000 Christians had been killed or, if they were fortunate, driven out, so that none remained in the town.

Attacks on other Christians in other towns followed.

It seems that persecutions persist, as do desperate times for believers. The flame flickers; it will flare again.

Devoted to Jude

AROUND the world, it's the nameless people, those who merely sign their initials on newspaper petitions, who created, and maintain, the legend of Jude. But the famous are ever ready to join them.

Towards the end of his long career, pool legend Minnesota Fats admitted he had almost lost a game once, about thirty years earlier. He faced the New Jersey hustler Lou Russo and was being beaten, but he said he called on "the patron saint of impossible propositions" and his record remained intact.

There is often a touch of humour in devotion to Jude. Sometimes it seems to be necessary.

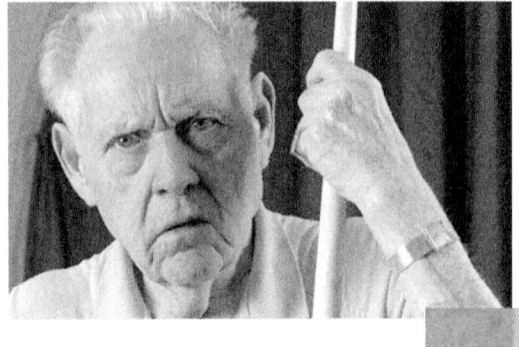

Above: Minnesota Fats had a sense of humour and great devotion to Jude.

Right: Bobby Nichols at 83, was still a Jude believer.

Below: Danny De Vito. The famous comedian always had a serious side when it came to Jude.

In 1964, golfer Bobby Nichols won the American PGA title, defeating Jack Nicklaus and Arnold Palmer by three strokes.

"I figured this was an impossible tournament to win," he said at the 19th hole. "I'm not superstitious. There's a difference between being superstitious and having faith. I have a lot of faith."

Nichols gave money from his winnings to establish a St Jude Shrine in Louisville, Kentucky.

Danny De Vito

Actor Danny De Vito visited the Jude shrine in Baltimore to pray and light candles while he was filming *Tin Men*. He was devoted to Jude.

There is a story told of the legendary Greta Garbo, who is said to have searched New York churches for a statue of Saint Jude. It's said that she found one at the Dominican Church of St Catherine in Manhattan. There she might well have discovered a steady procession of tearful souls coming from the nearby Sloan-Kettering Cancer Centre.

She might have read heartbreaking messages left at Jude's feet on scraps of paper.

In the 1950s, Lebanese-born comedian Danny Thomas gave the world the secret of his success. He

The legendary Greta Garbo searched high and low for a statue of St Jude, such was her faith.

Danny Thomas with a patient at St Jude Hospital

Danny Thomas with Elvis Presley. Elvis, and many other Hollywood stars were and are great supporters of St Jude Hospital.

St. Jude Children's
Research Hospital
ALSAC • Danny Thomas, Founder

was doing one-night stands in dingy clubs and hotels and finally prayed to St Jude for a big break. He got it and became a world-famous name. In gratitude, he built the St Jude Hospital for Children in Memphis, Tennessee.

Jamie Farr

Another Lebanese immigrant to America, Jamie Farr, of M*A*S*H fame, dedicated his autobiography to Jude as his way of thanking the saint and promoting his name. When he was unknown and living in a grubby basement apartment in Los Angeles, scratching to make ends meet, be began lighting candles at the Jude statue in his church. His big break came - in the film *The Greatest Story Ever Told*, playing the part, would you believe, of St Jude Thaddeus.

Jamie Farr went on to great success on stage and screen. He will be remembered for his role as Morrie, in *Tuesdays with Morrie*.

As well as famous people, other saints have demonstrated devotion to the Saint of the Impossible. In the fourteenth century, St Bridget (Brigitta) of Sweden, founder of the Order of the Most Holy Saviour, the Bridgettines, was devoted to Jude. Tradition says it was revealed to her by the Lord himself that Jude

St Jude's: The hospital Danny Thomas built.

Jamie Farr: Desperate, he prayed to Jude and landed his first real part—playing Saint Jude. He is remembered for roles as far apart as M*A*S*H and *Tuesdays with Morrie*.

would be "a powerful protector of those in desperate straits" and that she should turn to him with great confidence. Bridget said Jude "manfully fought the devil by the purity of his heart".

St Bernard of Clairvaux was involved with the planning of the Second Crusade. This was the last attempt to regain Edessa for Christianity. The holy war was doomed from the start and Bernard himself called the whole sorry campaign "an abyss too deep".

However, despite his difficulties, Bernard maintained a stout devotion to Jude throughout his life.

He had long revered a relic of the saint he had obtained from Jerusalem. When he died in 1153, the relic was buried with him "so that he might not be entirely without him whom, in life, he had found to be a powerful protector of his purity and a potent helper in every circumstance."

Praying to Jude

IN THE Sutro Library in California, there rests a treasure dating back to 1702. It is a worn, but precious sixteen-page Spanish novena to Saint Jude. This is but one example of prayer to the apostle flowing down through the ages.

Difficult times prompt renewed faith. Many novenas were started in churches around the world during the Second World War - as a plea for the return of loved ones. Jude's popularity soared again during the Korean and Vietnam wars, then in recent conflicts in

Iraq and Afghanistan and other places.

Prayers and novenas are a wonderful source of comfort, but some devotion is misplaced. Chain letters and novenas left on church pews sometimes offend with their wording - even though believers understand the desperation behind them. Some novenas, these days, are downloaded from the Internet.

"Make eighty one copies and leave nine copies in church for each of nine consecutive days. Your prayers will be answered before the nine days are over - no matter how impossible it may seem. This has never been known to fail." Hmm.

However, not all prayer is answered in the way we wish, and believers understand this. And believers also ignore the malicious overtones and direct threats that cause such offense with some chain letters. "If you ignore this chain letter, terrible misfortune will befall you."

They ignore this dark side to devotion and simply petition their patron saint with a prayer from the heart - and hope in him.

People implore the intercession of Jude in many ways. The following prayers appear in various versions in booklets, on holy cards, on novena sheets.

They are said for special occasions or as part of a novena to Jude. Other versions are readily available on the Internet.

Novenas are prayers said for nine days in succession and are considered a most potent method of petitioning the saint for help.

Short daily prayers to Saint Jude:

Oh, glorious apostle, St Jude Thaddeus, I salute you through the most Sacred Heart of Jesus. You who gloriously suffered martyrdom for the love of your divine Master, I beseech you, obtain for me the grace to remain always faithful to our Saviour, Jesus Christ. Amen.

Saint Jude, you were open to the Holy Spirit's loving energy. Help me to trust in God's care and to come to you when things seem hopeless. Amen.

Prayers to Saint Jude:

Any of these prayers may be used for a novena according to your needs:

Help for the Hopeless:

Holy Saint Jude - apostle and martyr, great in virtue, rich in miracles, near kinsman of Jesus Christ, faithful intercessor for all who invoke you, special patron in time of need - to you I fly from the depths of my heart, humbly begging you, to whom God has given such great power, to come to my assistance. Help me now in my urgent need; grant my earnest petition. I will never forget the grace and the favours you obtain for me, and I will do my best to spread devotion to you. Amen.

Blessed apostle, with confidence I invoke you. Saint Jude, Help of the Hopeless, aid me in my distress.

In the most desperate cases:

Glorious apostle, Saint Jude Thaddeus, true relative of Jesus and Mary, I greet you through the Sacred Heart of Jesus. Through this heart I praise and thank God for all the graces he has bestowed upon you. Humbly prostrate before you, I implore you, through this heart, to look down upon me with compassion. Despise not my poor prayers; let not my trust be wasted! God has granted you the privilege of aiding mankind in the most desperate cases. Come to my aid that I may praise the mercy of God! All my life I will be grateful to you and will be your faithful devotee until I can thank you in heaven. Amen.

For spiritual help:

Saint Jude Thaddeus, glorious apostle, martyr and relative of Jesus, you spread the true faith among the most barbarous and distant nations, and won to the obedience of Jesus Christ many tribes and peoples by the power of his holy word. Grant, I beseech you, that, from this day, I may renounce every sinful habit, be preserved from all evil thoughts, and always obtain your assistance, particularly in every danger and difficulty. May I safely reach our heavenly home and with you adore the most holy Trinity, Father, Son, and Holy Spirit, for ever and ever. Amen.

For things despaired of:

Most holy apostle Saint Jude, faithful servant and friend of Jesus, the name of the traitor who delivered your beloved Master into the hands of his enemies has caused you to be forgotten by many people. But the Church honours you and invokes you universally as the patron of hopeless cases and things despaired of. Pray for me; I am so helpless and alone. Make use, I implore you, of that particular privilege given to you of bringing visible and speedy help where help is almost despaired of. Come to my assistance in this great need and grant me the consolation and succour of heaven in all my necessities, tribulations, and sufferings, particularly... (here make your request...) *so that I may bless God with you and all the elect through eternity.*

I promise you, blessed Saint Jude, to be ever mindful of this great favour, and I will never cease to honour you as my special and powerful patron and to do all in my power to encourage devotion to you. Amen.

In grievous affliction:

Saint Jude Thaddeus - relative of Jesus and Mary, glorious apostle and martyr, renowned for your virtues and miracles, faithful and prompt intercessor of all who honour and trust in you, powerful patron and helper in grievous affliction - I come to you and entreat you with all my heart to come to my aid... (ask for the favour you require...), *for you have received from God the privilege of assisting with clear help those who almost despair.*

Look down upon me: my life is a life of crosses, my days full of tribulation, my paths strewn with thorns; scarcely one moment passes without witness to my tears and sighs. My soul is shrouded in darkness, disquietude, discouragement, mistrust; sometimes, even a kind of despair preys upon my soul. Divine providence seems lost to my sight and faith seems to falter in my heart. Overwhelmed by these thoughts, I see myself surrounded by a dark cloud. Do not forsake me in this sad plight! I will not leave you until you have heard me. Hasten to my aid. I will honour you as my special patron. I will thank God for the graces bestowed upon you, and will propagate your honour according to my power. Amen.

To obtain the love of God:

O glorious Saint Jude Thaddeus, by those sublime privileges which so ennobled you in your lifetime - your relationship according to the flesh with our Lord Jesus Christ, and your vocation to the apostolate - by that glory, which, as the reward of your labours and martyrdom, you now enjoy in heaven, obtain for me, from the giver of all good things, the spiritual and temporal favours I need.

Enable me to acquire the treasure of that divinely inspired doctrine which you have written about in your own

Help me raise on high the edifice of perfection upon the foundation of the faith, by prayer and the help of the Holy Spirit. Enable me to keep myself always in the love of God, waiting upon the mercy of Jesus Christ for life eternal, and to help by every available means those who stray from the truth. Thus shall I exalt the glory, the majesty, the dominion, the might of him who can preserve me from sin, and keep me stainless and joyous for the coming of my Lord Jesus Christ, my divine Saviour. Amen.

An act of thanksgiving:

O most sweet Lord, Jesus Christ, in union with the unutterable glory of the most holy Trinity that flows upon your sacred humanity, upon Mary and upon all the angels and saints, I praise, glorify and bless you for all the graces and privileges you have bestowed upon your chosen apostle and intimate friend, Jude Thaddeus. I pray you, for the sake of his merits, grant me your grace and, through his intercession, come to my aid in all my needs. Deign to strengthen me especially at the time of my death against the rage of my enemies. Amen.

Formal novena in honour of Saint Jude:

In the name of the Father and of the Son and of the Holy Spirit. Amen.

O Lord, Jesus Christ, who, when on earth, offered up prayer and entreaty, aloud and in silent tears to your Father, receive the offering of this novena, during which we desire to join our prayers to yours.

(Pray silently, and mention your petitions).

We make this offering through Mary, your Mother, and Saint Jude Thaddeus, your cousin, for he is our helper in difficult cases. For their sakes, accept and grant our prayer. Amen.

O glorious apostle, Saint Jude Thaddeus, Patron Saint of Hopeless Cases, who, when called by Jesus, left everything and followed Him, obtain for us the grace to detach ourselves from all worldly attachments to serve God, and to love our neighbour as we love ourselves.

Our Father, Hail Mary and Glory Be.

O faithful apostle, Saint Jude, beloved cousin of our Saviour, we admire the courage with which you spread the Gospel with great labours and sacrifices. Assist us so that we will never shirk our responsibility as Christians, and that we will practice daily by word and deed our faith.

Our Father, Hail Mary and Glory Be.

O zealous apostle, Saint Jude, who crowned your earthly life by martyrdom to give a true testimony of your faith, pray for us that we may imitate you in your great endurance, strengthen our weakness in time of temptation and help us to persevere in our faith so that with you one day we may come to glorify God forever. Amen.

Pray for us, Blessed Saint Jude, that we may be made worthy of the promises of Christ.

Father, you revealed yourself to us through the preaching of your apostle, Saint Jude. By his prayers give your church continued growth and increase the number of those who believe in you.

Grant this through our Lord Jesus Christ.

Litany to Saint Jude:
(For private devotion)

Lord, have mercy.
Christ, have mercy.
Lord, have mercy.
Christ, hear us,
Christ, graciously hear us.
God the Father of heaven, have mercy on us.

God the Son, redeemer of the world,

God the Holy Spirit,

Holy Trinity, one God,

St Jude, relative of Jesus and Mary, pray for us.

St Jude, while on earth deemed worthy to see Jesus and Mary, and to enjoy their company,

St Jude, raised to the dignity of an apostle,

St Jude, honoured in beholding the divine Master humble himself to wash your feet,

St Jude, who, at the Last Supper received the holy Eucharist from the hands of Jesus,

St Jude, who, after the profound grief which the death of your beloved Master caused you, had the consolation of beholding him risen from the dead, and of assisting at his glorious ascension,

St Jude, filled with the Holy Spirit on the day of Pentecost,

St Jude, who preached the gospel in Persia,

St Jude, who converted many people to the faith,

St Jude, who performed wonderful miracles in the power of the Holy Spirit,

St Jude, who restored an idolatrous king to health of both soul and body,

St Jude, who imposed silence on demons and really

confounded their oracles,

St Jude, who foretold to a prince an honourable peace with his powerful enemy.

St Jude, who took from deadly serpents the power of injuring man,

St Jude, who, disregarding the threats of the impious, courageously preached the doctrine of Christ,

St Jude, who gloriously suffered martyrdom for the love of your divine Master,

Blessed apostle, with confidence we invoke you!

(Three times)

St Jude, Help of the Hopeless, aid me in my distress!

(Three times)

That by your intercession, priests and people in the Church may obtain an ardent zeal for the faith of Jesus Christ, we beech you, hear us.

That you would defend our sovereign Pontiff and obtain peace and unity for the holy Church,

That all heathens and unbelievers may be converted to the true faith,

That faith, hope and charity may increase in our hearts,

That we may be delivered from evil thoughts and from the snares of the devil,

That you would deign to aid and protect all those who honour you,

That you would preserve us from all sin and all its occasions,

That you would defend us at the hour of death against the fury of the devil and of all evil spirits,

Pray for us, that, before death, we may expiate all our sins by sincere repentance and the worthy reception of the sacraments,

Pray for us, that we may appease divine justice and obtain a favourable judgment,

Pray for us, that we may be admitted into the company of the blessed, to rejoice in the presence of God forever,

Lamb of God, you take away the sins of the world, spare us, O Lord.

Lamb of God, you take away the sins of the world, graciously hear us, O Lord.

Lamb of God, you take away the sins of the world, have mercy on us.

St Jude, pray for us and for all who invoke your aid.

Sacrifice of the Holy Mass:
(Heard in honour of St Jude)

Catholics offer a triduum or novena of Masses (a Mass on three or nine consecutive days) and pray in these words:

O eternal Father, I offer you this holy sacrifice of your highest praise with the same love, humility and devotion, with the same intention and for the same end and aim as your beloved Son, the eternal High Priest, Jesus Christ himself, offers it to you. I offer it especially for the greater glory and beatitude of St Jude Thaddeus, in thanksgiving for all the graces and bliss bestowed upon him, and for my spiritual and temporal needs particularly for (here mention your special intentions). *Amen.*

But formal prayers are not the only way to reach Jude.

The man offering charitable works to Jude is reaching out to him. The woman in tears working her way down a church aisle on her knees is reaching out. So is a frightened child clutching a medal during an examination, or a patient doing the same while awaiting an operation.

For those in despair, there are sometimes no

words. Nor are they necessary. It is enough to simply open the heart in silence.

Indeed, when a mother in a children's hospital ward drags herself away from her terminally ill child and flops down in the hospital chapel, no words are possible.

For Jude, the whisper of a lost soul is enough.

Holy Shrines

MANY OF THE Jude faithful around the world have private shrines in their homes and gardens dedicated to their special saint. Jude statues, medals, holy cards and other articles of devotion are the first to sell out in many churches.

Farmers erect shrines in their fields.

But the shrines in churches large and small in many countries attract worshipers by the hundreds of thousands.

In Chile, those in need flock to a large shrine built by the Claretians in 1911.

There are several famous shrines in India - in the west at Mumbai (formerly Bombay), at Pakshikere,

Above: Saint Jude's in Sydney. Below: The Christian
Institute of Saint Jude, Khandwa, India.

Kemral Post, in southern India, and the most famous of all, Jhansi, in the heartland.

Jude is popular in India, particularly in the Anglo-Indian community. His "miracle stories" travelled quickly along the railway colonies, which had Anglo-Indians in high office. In Jhansi, in Madhya Pradesh, pilgrims from all over India now flock to the Shrine of St Jude.

Many of India's thirty million Christians turn to Jude in times of religious intolerance and try to make the pilgrimage to one of his shrines.

Nuns tell the story of a man in Sri Lanka, who severely injured his back and could neither walk nor work.

Hopeless Situation

He considered his situation hopeless. In desperation, he asked friends to carry him to a small Jude shrine in the mountains. His recovery began and soon he was back at work. The man had no doubt where he should place the credit for his recovery.

Stories such as these are common-place wherever talk turns to Jude.

The priests of the Capuchin Franciscan Fraternity at Leichhardt, in Australia, run a kind of shrine-by-mail. Petition forms, novena leaflets, booklets and medals are available from their office.

They invite petitions and thanksgiving letters, offerings and enquiries. The petitions are placed near a relic of Saint Jude and prayed for. Thanksgiving letters often detail intervention by Jude in the lives of the faithful, whether they be considered miracles or Jude's "coincidences".

Many shrines publish newsletters to keep in touch with believers. In Rome, a Carmelite shrine to Saint Jude publishes a newsletter called *The Voice of the Apostle - St Jude Thaddeus*. But, one way or another, believers try to get to the shrine. There they gather and exchange stories of interventions and miracles by their beloved Jude.

A road from Turkey enters Iran at Gurbulak, a few miles east of Dogubeyazit. People with an Iranian visa can make a day trip to a magnificent Armenian Monastery of Saint Thaddeus. From here, there are magnificent views of Mount Ararat and some of the territory covered by Jude on his missionary journeys.

But no other country has as many shrines as America.

There are shrines in San Diego, in Washington, in Westchester County, in Louisville, Kentucky. A shrine is run by the Franciscans at Mt Vernon, New York.

Parish of Hope

St Stephen's Church in New York calls itself the "Parish of Hope" and the "National Shrine of Saint Jude" - a claim also made in Chicago and Washington.

The National Shrine in Chicago, erected in 1925, receives hundreds of thousands of petitions every year. It is operated by the Claretian Fathers at Our Lady of Guadalupe Church. The priests publish *Saint Jude's Journal* and *The Voice of Saint Jude,* which publishes many answered petitions.

A second shrine in Chicago is operated by the Dominicans at the Church of Saint Pius.

The shrine in St John the Baptist Church in downtown Baltimore has half a million names on its mailing list. It receives five hundred letters a week containing petitions, thanks and donations. Here, as elsewhere, many believers who cannot travel reach out for Jude by mail.

A Million Petitions

There is a shrine in San Francisco, called "The Shrine of the West", run by the Dominicans at Saint Dominic's Church. The shrine was erected during the Great Depression and now draws more than a million people to petition in person or by letter every year.

In its files, as in the shrine files everywhere, there are stories of miracles and interventions.

A priest's niece, so the story goes, fell pregnant and developed serious health problems. Doctors wanted to abort the pregnancy, but the woman risked her life - and the baby's - by continuing the pregnancy. She prayed to Jude and both mother and baby survived. Another woman, in desperation, applied Saint Jude Oil to a baby that had drowned - and the baby recovered.

Wherever people talk of Jude, they talk of the miracles, the interventions, the "Jude coincidences" in their lives or those of their friends.

At shrines, people light votive candles and leave scraps of paper containing their petitions and torments.

Bridal bouquets are left at the foot of Jude statues for a happy marriage. Couples in their wedding outfits kneel before the statues. Others strew flowers at the saint's feet.

Sometimes a flower or a scrap of paper can say what the tongue cannot.

Petitions and Thanks

ONE OF THE traditions that has grown as part of the legend of Saint Jude is that, in return for favours granted, petitioners should promote Jude's name wherever they can and thank him publicly.

One of the easiest ways to accomplish both is to use the Public Notices section of newspapers, or, these days, on the Internet. Hence, around the world, notices of petition and thanks now appear regularly in newspapers large and small.

Newspaper offices are often asked for the wording of Jude prayers. Here is a selection of prayers that have appeared in various newspapers (as usual, most petitioners prefer to use initials, rather than full names):

In American newspapers (including the New York Times, the New York Post, the Village Voice, the San Francisco Chronicle and the International Herald-Tribune):

Saint Jude's Novena: May the Sacred Heart of Jesus be adored, glorified, loved and preserved throughout the world, now and forever. Sacred Heart of Jesus, have mercy on us. Saint Jude, worker of miracles, pray for us. Saint Jude, helper of the hopeless, pray for us. Thank you.

G.A.H.

Saint Jude, worker of miracles, thank you for all the miracles, help and protection given when I called your name.

P.B.K. and family.

Pray to Saint Jude, patron of things despaired of, intercessor of all who invoke his special patronage in time of need. Saint Jude will help you in present and urgent petition. I prayed to Saint Jude - a miracle took place. The same can happen for you. Thank you, Saint Jude, for answering my prayer.

P.J.

O Holy Spirit, Infant Jesus, Saint Jude, worker of miracles, I thank you for favours received. Continue showering your blessing on me. C.M.

Saint Jude - apostle, martyr, relative of Jesus Christ - intercede for us. Thank you for prayers answered. T.R.P.

In India (including The Times of India and Mid Day Mumbai):

Thank you, Saint Jude, for many favours received. Jude please continue to intercede for us. Thanks for the cure of my sister. W.X.

My long-delayed thanks to Saint Jude for granting me a very great favour. E.Fonseca.

Thanks to Saint Jude for all favours received. Continue to guide us always. Published as promised. Flavy.

Thank you, Saint Jude, for cure of mother and good job. Protect us. Rego.

Grateful thanks to Saint Jude for saving my life. S.P.

Thanks to Saint Jude for the safe delivery of a baby boy. J.R.

In Australia (including the Sydney Morning Herald, the Daily Telegraph, the Macarthur Advertiser, the Liverpool Champion and the Wentworth Courier):

Oh holy Saint Jude, apostle and martyr, I have recourse to you from the depths of my heart. I humbly beg you, to whom God has given such great powers, to come to my assistance. Help me now in this present and urgent need and grant my earnest petition. Saint Jude, pray for me. Thank you for helping me. Jennifer.

Thank you, Saint Jude, for favours granted. Continue to bless me and my family. B.O.N.

Thank you, Saint Jude, for everything. C.T.

Thank you Saint Jude, for a positive medical report for my daughter. Bless us always. T.A.

Saint Jude, thank you for your miracle. I will pray to you always. B.M.

Thank you, Saint Jude, for your intercession. I am so grateful. It has changed my life. Z.N.E.

In England (including the Daily Mirror, the Times, the Birmingham Post, Manchester Evening News):

Thank you, Saint Jude, for the successful operation on our mother. Praised be the name of Jesus. May he always bless our families with good health. Published as promised. George R.

Thank you, Saint Jude, for favours granted. We love you and continue to pray fervently. T.M.P.

Saint Jude, thank you for examination help. Bless you. S.F.

Thank you Saint Jude's Novena. Thank you, Saint Jude, for prayer answered. C.N.

Eternal gratitude to Saint Jude for saving my baby's life. C.S.

May the Blessed Saviour be praised. Thank you, Saint

Jude, for the favour only you know about. P.T.D.

Sometimes the longer prayers set out earlier in this book are used in these notices, but shorter notices are easier on the pocket for many. Often just a single line serves the purpose: it spreads the word and gives thanks.

Flame of Hope

WHEN JUDE fanned the flame of hope two thousand years ago, he was a lonely man battling despair, strange gods, strange customs, acts of betrayal and barbarism, mortal danger and a feeling of shame for having deserted Jesus.

The flame flickered in times of turbulence, but always flared again in the hearts of believers, and it began to spread around the world - wherever there was a need for an antidote to despair.

It spread through Russia, Poland, Czechoslovakia, Brazil, Mexico, Cuba, Costa Rica, Chile, Peru - to all the peoples of Central and South America. It spread throughout Europe, to Australia, to India, to the Philippines.

It spread to questing hearts everywhere.

In Australia, priests of the Society of St Paul spread devotion to Jude, based on the miracles he has performed.

"St Jude Thaddeus shows his special help and protection in those circumstances which are deemed most difficult and desperate," the priests say in a booklet. "St Jude has restored health to those stricken with sickness which defied all human skill and remedies. The holy apostle obtains help in anguish, distress, calumny, poverty, misery, yes, even in despair and in circumstances where aid seems utterly impossible."

Battle with Despair

People in the front line of the day-to-day battle with despair proclaim their faith in Jude, based on first-hand knowledge. People like Father Leonard, Procurator of Jude devotion with the Capuchin Franciscan Fraternity in Leichhardt, Sydney, who receives letters of thanks from all over Australia. Like the nuns at St Joseph's Centre for Care in Croydon, where, for one hundred and fifty years, children in need of urgent rescue from "violent and dangerous situations" are taken in - along with children with disabilities, from toddlers up. They know full well the value of St Jude to the destitute. So does Glen McNamara, who runs St Jude's Refuge for Men in Bankstown.

Pat Peebles, who runs St Jude's Nurses Agency in Randwick, named her business after her special patron.

"Jude has been very good to me," she said. "Over many years, my prayers have always been answered. The answer is not always what I want or when I want it - but my prayers are always answered."

Humour and Jude

Despite the serious nature of most devotion to Jude, there is often a great deal of humour associated with him.

Pat Peebles wrote to the National Shrine in Chicago and obtained a statue of Jude, which sits in her office.

"Whenever business is slow," she says with a laugh, "I kind of glare at him - and someone always comes through the door."

A Mumbai woman, Mrs Wakeman, always had

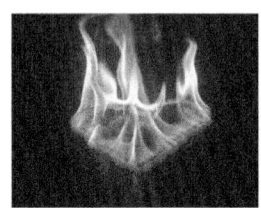

The flame of hope burns bright still, just
as it did years ago for this patient of
Saint Jude Children's Hospital and the
man who gave her hope,
Danny Thomas.

her "brood" praying to St Jude for various things. One of her daughters threatened to hang St Jude upside down outside her window if she didn't find a beau. Jude apparently enjoys a joke, because the loveless lass ended up with a stream of suitors.

Miracle? Jude "coincidence"? For believers, it doesn't matter. When they pray to Jude, many simply expect something to happen and, when it does, they assume Jude has intervened.

Novena to Saint Jude

Anthony and Natalina D'Souza, from Goa, in the south of India, were childless for seven years. Nattie tried various therapies to become pregnant and consulted specialists, but her case, she was told, was hopeless. A friend, Motti Mama (meaning, so I'm told, Fat Aunt), gave Nattie a novena to St Jude. The desperate woman made the novena. She conceived and named her baby girl Judith, after Jude.

Judith now lives in Australia with her husband and two children.

Nattie also appealed to Jude (and St Anthony) years later, when she lost her wedding ring on the way to hospital. A schoolgirl found the ring and handed it to the Reverend Mother at St Mary of the

Angels' School in Rajasthan. This happened to be the school where Judith studied and another relative taught. The ring was returned to Nattie.

Clutched a Medal

Some people are shy about having their names published. A Sydney woman was diagnosed with terminal cancer. She had workmates who prayed to Jude for her. She was not a Christian herself, but clutched a Jude medal given to her by a friend. She has amazed doctors, and herself, and there is now no sign of cancer. Friends are grateful to St Jude, but not entirely surprised.

Two women, on opposite sides of Australia, were also diagnosed with terminal cancer - a wife and mother in Perth and a nun in Sydney. Both had friends who prayed to Jude.

The Perth woman was swamped with an avalanche of prayers from around Australia and overseas. The nun had fellow nuns, students and friends praying. It was "touch and go", but both women now appear to have beaten the disease and are "in remission".

Such stories are common-place at shrines around the world. Read them for yourself; many are online.

A few years ago, Cynthia Goudie made it into the

media for all the wrong reasons when she was hit by a truck in Melbourne. The impact broke her neck in three places, fractured her pelvis and compressed her spinal cord.

Her husband, Ian, phoned friends in Australia and America to pray for her. Cynthia had already seen faith cure a friend's cancer that was supposedly incurable. For the crippled woman, the road to recovery was long, involving operations and extensive treatment - and she never fully recovered.

But she was not a quadriplegic. She could walk and talk and lead a normal life. And she had no doubt that prayer had worked a miracle in her life. Nor had one of the friends, who showed the author the newspaper clipping and laid the credit directly at the feet of Jude.

Man with a Mission

Father Denis Madigan was a chaplain with the Ambulance Service in Australia and author of a newspaper column called *Man with a Mission*.

"I often have letters and stories from people who have nothing but thanks for the apostle Jude," Father Madigan said.

"A friend, who calls on St Jude for support, says

the apostle never failed him in his exams, and he had no doubt St Jude would help him again when his death sentence' was passed. At 34, with a happy family and excellent job prospects, my friend learnt he had cancer, which would need nine hours of surgery, with only a twenty per cent success rate. The surgery was successful."

Life Saved Twice

A man well-known to the author credits St Jude with saving his life twice. This man prays regularly to Jude for others, but never for himself.

"I think Jude's got better things to do than to worry about me," he says.

For many years, he had a black mark on his forehead, near the hairline, about three centimetres (an inch) in diameter. One day, without knowing why, he had an urge to talk to his doctor about it while in the surgery on another matter. The doctor said it was common, that nothing need be done about it unless it changed colour or size, and that probably wouldn't happen for many years, if at all.

The man persisted.

"If it did turn nasty, how long would I have?"

The doctor said that, if it was malignant and had

started to "travel", he would have to do something about it within a fortnight because of the spot's location - otherwise it could spread quickly into the glandular system and, at that time, nothing could be done.

"Doc," said the patient, "I'm colour-blind. Cut the damn thing out now."

A week later, in hospital, the surgery was done. A fortnight later, in his surgery, the doctor said there had been some kind of mix-up, that the biopsy report had not come. He phoned for the report. The man, to this day, remembers the blood draining from the doctor's face when he heard the cancer had been both malignant and moving.

Jude was there

The man believes Jude had a hand in his sudden urge to do something about his long-running skin cancer, even though he had not asked for help.

Some years before that, the man did pray to Jude for himself - just once. He had been diagnosed with having had "six or eight" myocardial infarctions (small heart attacks). He was ordered complete rest on a range of medications, including little pills to slip under his tongue to relieve pressure on his chest, and Valium. He can't remember the others. Finally, in utter frustration, he cried out silently to Jude.

"There's no way words can tell you what happened," he says. "Suddenly, my chest felt as if it was expanding at a rapid rate - almost to the bursting point. And my heart... it was thumping almost out of my chest. I was terrified. But, in a matter of a minute or two, I think, I suddenly felt a great surge in the heart, a release, as if a blockage had been cleared. The surge spread through my body, as if the blood could suddenly flow again. In minutes, it was all over. My chest was relaxed, the heartbeat - well, I couldn't feel it. I was exhausted, but I can't tell you how good I felt. What did the doc say? I didn't tell him. How could I?"

Twenty years later, that man claims his heart is as strong as a horse. And he knows who made it that way.

As long as Jude lives in the hearts of believers, so does hope.

THROUGHOUT the ages, people have suffered. No-one is immune from life's calamities. Poverty, sickness, betrayal, injustice, cruelty, pain, loneliness, heartache... at one time or another, such things touch us all. We have to cope, or we sink into despair.

Jude lived in tough times. So do we. Sometimes we are in our own Gethsemane. Sometimes we need a tough saint.

Where do you turn when an examination is looming and you know how much you don't know, or can't remember - and yet your future, your honour, depends on the result?

Where do you turn when you are stricken with an illness, with pain, that will not go away? When doctors and the wonders of science can do nothing for you... when life is ebbing away and no-one can stop the flow?

Where do you turn when your marriage or family breaks up? When you lose your job, your business fails, you lose your self-esteem, your courage fails you?

Where Do You Turn?

Where do you turn when an earthquake strikes, or a flood, a tidal wave, fire, famine? Where do you turn when these things wipe away your home, your children, your parents, your loved ones?

Where do you turn when you are a child and you

are starving? Where do you turn when you are on death row? When you are a refugee... when you have seen bloodshed and cruelty and merciless death... when you have no-where to go and no-one to go to?

Where do you turn when you are in despair... in deep depression? When hope is gone and you have lost your faith, or when you had none to start with?

Believers can tell you.

You turn to Jude. Saint of the Impossible. Patron of Desperate Cases. Hope of the Hopeless.

Abraham Lincoln used to say that, when he had exhausted all possibilities and he had no-where else to go, he would go down on his knees.

The Medicine of Hope

And there, on your knees, please God, you will find the help only hope can give - for hope is the only medicine to heal the miserable. There, please God, you will find a miracle.

You might not think you deserve it, but you are human and something bad is happening to you - and that is where Jude comes into his own. He is at his best when the weather is foul.

Those who have no need, have no need of Jude. Those who need, need Jude.

People by the thousand, by the million, around the world, have found this to be so. To them, Jude is a mystery, a marvellous gift from a God who knows the lowly sometimes need an intermediary to approach him. Someone close to him. Someone with a big heart. Someone like Jude.

He was not a prophet. The Jews gave him no honours or authority whatever. He never achieved high office, never received the symbols of priesthood - but he was chosen by Jesus himself to be an apostle.

And no-one who came before him or after him on this earth - except for Jesus Christ and his mother - has been so beloved and so venerated by the poor, the sick, the downtrodden, the desperate.

Jude's flame of hope, say believers, is the eternal flame they will never allow to die.

And so, the legend of Jude continues...

###

A Final Word

IF YOU LIKED this book, could I ask you to do something for me to help promote it and Jude? I wrote both this book and *The Life of Jude: Saint of the Impossible* for believers everywhere, but I need help to let them know about the books.

The books cannot be found in bookstores (unless they are ordered in), but can be found online at amazon.com. (Bookstores, shrines and other outlets who would like to stock the book can do so, and should contact me if they have a problem). Meanwhile, I have to find a way to let people know the books exist, and you might be able to help me.

One of the best ways to promote books these

days is to go to amazon.com, search for the books by title, and leave a review or comment or a few words to help people decide whether to buy or not. My website has links to the books if anyone has trouble.

Any mention in social networks or book clubs and so on would also be very helpful. I'm sure you know more about spreading the word to friends, and I'm sure you'd be more comfortable talking about my book than I am.

I'd also like to hear from you for whatever reason. You can contact me directly at any time on brianmorganbooks@gmail.com.

Thank you for reading and for any support you can give. I worked for more than 50 years on these two books, so you'll understand that I'm very keen to promote Jude to believers everywhere. If you are a believer, you will also be keen to promote him.

By all means, contact me or visit my website at www.brianmorganbooks.com. Thank you again, and I look forward to hearing from you.

Brian.

About the Author

BRIAN MORGAN is an award-winning, best-selling writer, who is dedicating the senior years of his life to inspiring and motivating people through his books and other writings.

He has been described as a business and thought leader, a business founder, an integrity advocate, a national award-winning journalist, editor and publisher, and an internationally acclaimed author.

He has been honoured by his community on numerous occasions for his long years of service to various community groups and organisations.

In 2012, in association with The Writers Trust, he commenced a program to publish all of his books in print and as eBooks. All the details can be found on his website.

Brian's new mission in life is summed up in his site's logo: *Stories to Touch Lives*.

Printed in Great Britain
by Amazon